My Father and Me

My Father and Me

ROBIN NOEL TALBOT

Xulon Press

Xulon Press
2301 Lucien Way #415
Maitland, FL 32751
407.339.4217
www.xulonpress.com

© 2023 by Robin Noel Talbot

All rights reserved solely by the author. The author guarantees all contents are original and do not infringe upon the legal rights of any other person or work. No part of this book may be reproduced in any form without the permission of the author.

Due to the changing nature of the Internet, if there are any web addresses, links, or URLs included in this manuscript, these may have been altered and may no longer be accessible. The views and opinions shared in this book belong solely to the author and do not necessarily reflect those of the publisher. The publisher therefore disclaims responsibility for the views or opinions expressed within the work.

Paperback ISBN-13: 978-1-66287-653-0
Hard Cover ISBN-13: 978-1-66287-654-7
Ebook ISBN-13: 978-1-66287-655-4

For my boys, Patrick and Sean

"How's the view up there?" I asked.

What do you see down there? he wondered.

Lift me up! I thought.

"Hop on my shoulders," he said.

The trees grew smaller as I grew taller

Up on my father's shoulders.

Hold on tight, I thought.

"Reach for the sky," he said.

Don't fall, I thought.

"I'll always catch you," he said.

Time passed by,

We both reached for the sky.

Many times I fell.

He always caught me.

I reached again

And this time he fell.

How does he do it? I wondered.

How do you do it? he thought.

Is he in pain? I wondered.

Are you in pain? he wondered.

"Dad, why are you sick?" I asked.

"Don't stop reaching," he said.

"But why, Dad?" I asked.

"The world is waiting for you," he said.

"You're too young," I said.

"You're so young," he said.

"Who will catch me when you're gone?" I asked.

"You're a fine young boy," he said.

He closed his eyes.

A teardrop rolled down his cheek.

I closed my eyes.

Teardrops rolled down my cheeks.

He took one last breath

And he was gone.

Time passed by,

I reached for the sky.

How's the view up there? I wondered.

What do you see down there? he wondered.